JUSTICE RISING

12 Amazing Black Women
in the Civil Rights Movement

Written by
Katheryn Russell-Brown

Illustrated by
Kim Holt

VIKING

An imprint of Penguin Random House LLC, New York

First published in the United States of America by Viking,
an imprint of Penguin Random House LLC, 2023

Text copyright © 2023 by Katheryn Russell-Brown
Illustrations copyright © 2023 by Kim Holt

Visit us online at penguinrandomhouse.com.

Library of Congress Cataloging-in-Publication Data is available.

Manufactured in China

ISBN 9780593403549

1 3 5 7 9 10 8 6 4 2

TOPL

Edited by Liza Kaplan • Design by Monique Sterling

Text set in Recoleta and Adobe Caslon Pro

Artwork created with digital paint and paper texture.

FREEDOM NOW!!

FIGHT

EQUAL RIGHTS

To my children, Louis and Sasha

— K. R. B.

To my family, who has cheered me on and encouraged me
to always be courageous and step out on faith

— K. H.

A Movement Takes Shape

The US Civil Rights Movement, which lasted from the 1950s through the 1960s, was a time of great upheaval, protest, and change. A movement happens when a large group of people set goals and take actions to meet those goals. Thousands of Black people, mostly from the American South, were determined to fight for equality and justice. Black women, in particular, were the backbone of the Civil Rights Movement. They knew that every person could do something—big or small—to create a better world. Black women were involved in every part of the movement. There was so much work to do. Some women organized marches, others wrote letters to protest segregation, and some arranged meetings to discuss voting rights. Some of them believed so strongly in racial justice that they quit their jobs, moved away from home, or quit school to join the Civil Rights Movement. They decided to use their voices and their feet to do something. And yet, even though Black women did the majority of the work, most of them did not receive credit for their contributions.

This book includes the stories of twelve *she*roes of the Civil Rights Movement. Each woman played her own special part. Each believed that it was unfair to treat people differently because of their skin color. One thing is certain: no matter how hard the road was to achieve racial equality, these women kept fighting for justice.

SAY THEIR NAMES!

1. Ella Baker
2. Ruby Bridges
3. Claudette Colvin
4. Dorothy Cotton
5. Fannie Lou Hamer
6. Coretta Scott King
7. Diane Nash
8. Rosa Parks
9. Bernice Johnson Reagon
10. Gloria Richardson
11. Jo Ann Robinson
12. Sheyann Webb
13. Freedom Marchers

Ella Baker

1903–1986 • Norfolk, Virginia

Growing up, Ella saw that women had the power to change the world. She watched her mother work with other women to teach and help people.

Like her mother, Ella wasn't afraid to speak her mind.

After college, Ella joined different groups to help women and Black people gain rights. She knew how to organize people to work for justice. Ella was successful because she listened when people talked and she cared about everyday folks.

In the 1960s, when students started sit-ins at lunch counters, Ella met with student leaders. She realized that young people needed a bigger voice in the Civil Rights Movement. She helped start the Student Nonviolent Coordinating Committee.

Ella is revered as the mother of the Civil Rights Movement.

Ruby Bridges

1954– • Tylertown, Mississippi

First grade! Ruby was excited to begin school. Each day, tall men wearing suits with badges walked with her to the schoolhouse door. Ruby and the men passed by large crowds of people who hollered threats and carried signs telling her to go home. They didn't want her to integrate the school. Ruby hugged her books tight, held her head high, and walked ahead.

Inside the building, Ruby felt safe. She had her very own teacher, Mrs. Henry. There were no other students in the classroom because White parents didn't want their children in school with a Black child.

Just by going to school, six-year-old Ruby made a difference. Sometimes doing something ordinary can change the world.

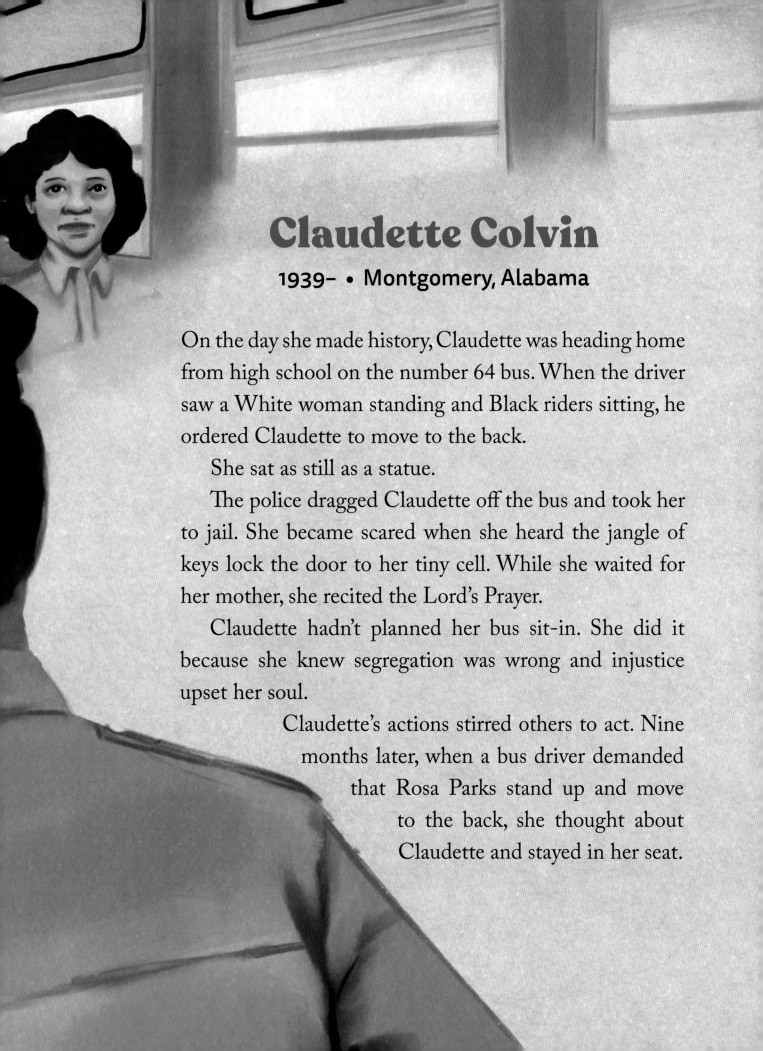

Claudette Colvin

1939– • Montgomery, Alabama

On the day she made history, Claudette was heading home from high school on the number 64 bus. When the driver saw a White woman standing and Black riders sitting, he ordered Claudette to move to the back.

She sat as still as a statue.

The police dragged Claudette off the bus and took her to jail. She became scared when she heard the jangle of keys lock the door to her tiny cell. While she waited for her mother, she recited the Lord's Prayer.

Claudette hadn't planned her bus sit-in. She did it because she knew segregation was wrong and injustice upset her soul.

Claudette's actions stirred others to act. Nine months later, when a bus driver demanded that Rosa Parks stand up and move to the back, she thought about Claudette and stayed in her seat.

Dorothy Cotton

1930–2018 • Goldsboro, North Carolina

"There's your ready girl!" That's how Miss Gray described Dorothy, her star English student. Whatever the task, Dorothy was prepared.

Growing up, it bothered Dorothy that Black people couldn't use the public library. When she became a civil rights activist, Dorothy worked to make the laws fair. After hearing Dr. Martin Luther King Jr. give a speech, she moved to Atlanta to lead the Citizenship Education Program. The program taught thousands of Black people how to read, write, and register to vote.

Dorothy became the only woman to serve on Dr. King's leadership team. She knew how to organize people and get things done. She helped plan the Children's Crusade and the St. Augustine march.

Dorothy was always ready to work for justice.

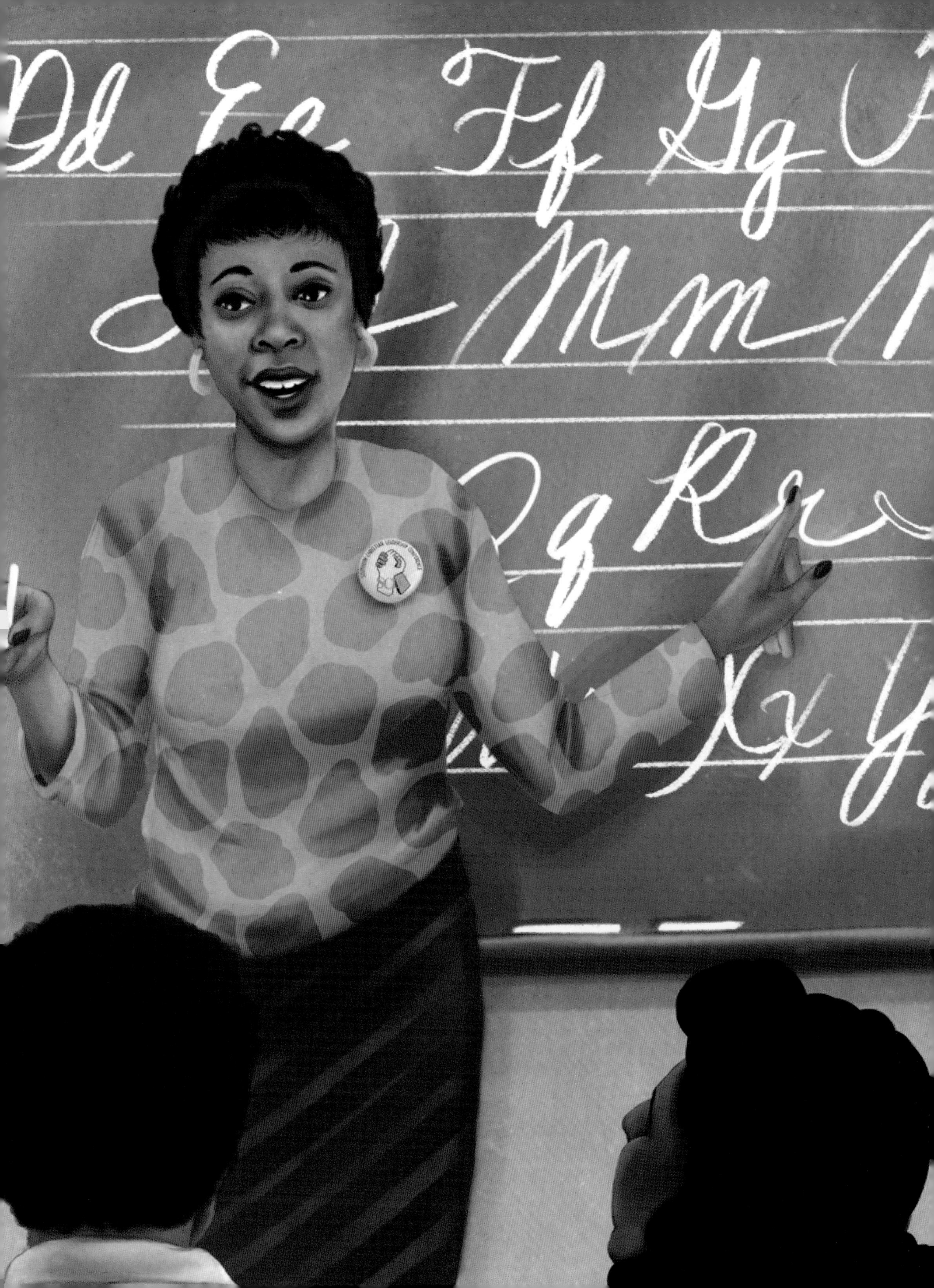
Dd Ff Gg
Mm
Qq Rr
Xx

Fannie Lou Hamer

1917–1977 • Montgomery County, Mississippi

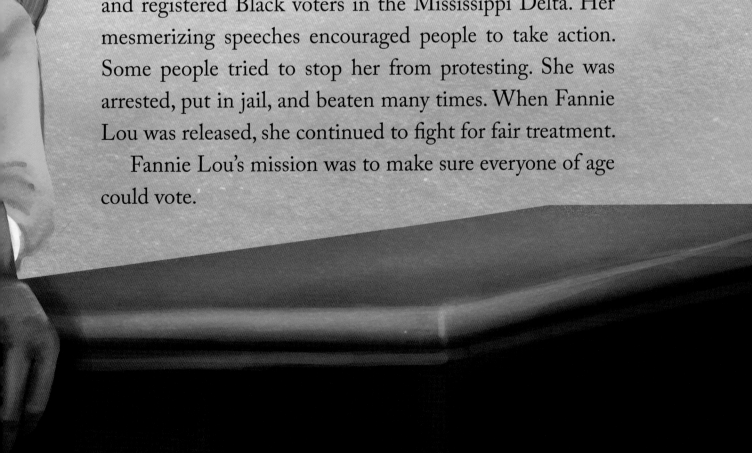

Young Fannie Lou loved school. But she had to quit after sixth grade to help her family. They needed Fannie Lou—the youngest of twenty children—to help pick cotton. It was especially tough work for Fannie Lou, who suffered polio when she was six.

Years later, at age forty-four, Fannie Lou learned that Black people had voting rights. When her boss heard that she planned to vote, he fired Fannie Lou and forced her off his plantation.

Fannie Lou then joined the Civil Rights Movement and registered Black voters in the Mississippi Delta. Her mesmerizing speeches encouraged people to take action. Some people tried to stop her from protesting. She was arrested, put in jail, and beaten many times. When Fannie Lou was released, she continued to fight for fair treatment.

Fannie Lou's mission was to make sure everyone of age could vote.

Coretta Scott King

1927–2006 • Heiberger, Alabama

Coretta's family knew firsthand that some people hated others based on the color of their skin. Coretta learned early that no matter what happened, she had to keep pushing forward.

At age ten, Coretta and her sister picked cotton in the hot sun to pay for school.

In college, Coretta worked with civil rights groups. She spoke up when she saw injustice.

When she married Martin Luther King Jr., they became civil rights partners. Coretta helped plan events and performed Freedom Concerts to raise money.

After Martin was killed, Coretta's heart was heavy. But she continued to speak against war and poverty. She built a center for nonviolence and organized a holiday for Dr. King.

Coretta knew the fight for justice would be long. So she kept fighting.

Diane Nash

1938– • Chicago, Illinois

Diane was twenty-one when she moved to Nashville for college. Everywhere she looked there were WHITES ONLY and COLOREDS ONLY signs. She was furious. Jim Crow laws made it legal to treat people differently based on their skin color. They made the world small for Black people.

She had to do something. Diane studied how to use nonviolence to fight for equality and became a peace activist.

Diane was arrested many times for organizing civil rights marches and sit-ins. She was even arrested when she was six months pregnant. The judge sentenced her to ten days in jail.

To show that segregation was wrong, Diane helped organize Freedom Riders. Hundreds of Black and White students rode together on buses traveling through the Deep South. The Riders were attacked by violent mobs. Still, Diane refused to let that stop the Freedom Riders.

Diane believed that peaceful protest was the only answer to violence.

Rosa Parks

1913–2005 • Tuskegee, Alabama

Ten-year-old Rosa didn't let anybody treat her like a second-class citizen. When she was bullied by a White boy, she threatened him with a rock. She was raised to have pride.

As an adult, Rosa joined groups pushing for equal rights. She especially wanted a fair world for Black women.

Rosa was determined to vote, even though the rules weren't fair. Black people had to take a test and White people didn't. Rosa took the test again and again until finally, she passed on her third try.

Segregation made Rosa feel sad. One day on her bus ride home, she refused to move to let a White man sit down. Rosa's arrest was news around the world and sparked a year-long bus boycott in Montgomery, Alabama.

Rosa fought for civil rights every day of her life.

Bernice Johnson Reagon

1942– • Dougherty County, Georgia

Bernice was a preacher's daughter who started singing when she was little. Growing up, she sang in the church choir and all through school. When a piano wasn't available, the choir sang a capella. Bernice preferred that sound. Just voices.

In college, Bernice joined with students who wanted equality. Whenever they marched—at churches, police stations, and courthouses—they sang freedom songs. Bernice was the song leader. She knew dozens of songs and always picked the right one to energize or calm down the crowd.

Bernice was expelled from college for protesting. So she enrolled at another school and kept on singing for justice.

Gloria Richardson

1922–2021 • Baltimore, Maryland

They called her "Glorious Gloria." Some said she was a modern-day Harriet Tubman. In the same county where Tubman had been enslaved, Gloria planned demonstrations to demand jobs and schools for Black people. Gloria was fierce. At one march, when a national guardsman pointed his bayonet at her, she pushed it away.

In 1963, after months of protests and unrest, the Treaty of Cambridge was signed—an agreement between Gloria's organization, the Cambridge Nonviolent Action Committee, and the city of Cambridge, Maryland.

Gloria's work helped to desegregate the city and pushed Congress to pass the 1964 Civil Rights Act.

Jo Ann Robinson

1912–1992 • Culloden, Georgia

Jo Ann Robinson had a troubling experience riding the bus in Montgomery, Alabama. When the driver saw that Jo Ann wasn't sitting in the back, he screamed at her and kicked her off the nearly empty bus. Tears rolled down her face.

A year later, Jo Ann became president of the Women's Political Council. She demanded that bus drivers stop bullying Black riders and fought against unfair seating rules.

When Rosa Parks was arrested in 1955, Jo Ann's group was ready. Overnight they printed thousands of flyers, encouraging Black people to stop riding segregated buses. For thirteen months, thousands of Black people walked and shared rides during the Montgomery Bus Boycott, until finally, the Supreme Court ruled segregation on buses was unconstitutional.

Jo Ann was a leader in the Civil Rights Movement's most successful boycott.

Sheyann Webb

1956– • Selma, Alabama

On her walk to school one morning, eight-year-old Sheyann saw Black and White people talking in front of Brown Chapel AME. For Selma in 1965, this was a strange sight. Curious, Sheyann went inside and sat down. For five hours, speakers talked about voting rights for Black people.

At home, Sheyann told Momma what she'd learned: "If you can't vote, you're not free."

Sheyann continued to skip school and attend meetings. When Dr. King visited the church, she met him.

In 1965, civil rights leaders planned the Selma to Montgomery March to support voting rights. Sheyann was determined to be there. At the march, police attacked protestors with nightsticks and tear gas. Sheyann ran home as fast as she could. Tear gas burned her eyes. She was so scared, that night she wrote her obituary.

Dr. King called Sheyann the "smallest freedom fighter."

Freedom Marchers

A movement wouldn't be a movement without public protest marches. Marches were held in front of courthouses, monuments, and jails. The marchers walked, carried signs, sang songs, and demanded positive change.

Black women worked tirelessly on the front lines and behind the scenes to make sure the civil rights marches were successful. They did whatever had to be done. They wrote speeches, cooked food, passed out flyers, and made phone calls. Civil rights marches made news around the world. Everyone heard about the March on Washington, the Selma to Montgomery March, and the Children's Crusade.

These Black women, and the people they inspired, worked to ensure justice for all.

Quotes

"People cannot be free until there is enough work in this land to give everybody a job."
—Ella Baker

"Racism is a grown-up disease. Let's stop using our kids to spread it." —Ruby Bridges

"We had been studying the Constitution . . . I knew I had rights." —Claudette Colvin

"Nonviolence provided grounding, a base from which we could struggle for justice."
—Dorothy Cotton

"I'm sick and tired of being sick and tired." —Fannie Lou Hamer

"I am not a ceremonial symbol. I am an activist." —Coretta Scott King

"Freedom, by definition, is people realizing that they are their own leaders." —Diane Nash

"Freedom fighters never retire." —Rosa Parks

"Freedom songs are documents created by a collective voice." —Bernice Johnson Reagon

"A first-class citizen does not beg for freedom." —Gloria Richardson

"Something had to be done." —Jo Ann Robinson

"My feet and legs may be tired, but my soul still feels like marchin'." —Sheyann Webb

Sources

ELLA BAKER

"Ella Baker—'The Mother of the Civil Rights Movement.'" Hosted by Henry Louis Gates Jr.
Black History in Two Minutes or So, March 13, 2020. Video, 3:01. youtube.com
/watch?v=McneFCdHUn0.

"Founding of SNCC." Digital SNCC Gateway. snccdigital.org/events/founding-of-sncc.

Grant, Joanne, dir. *Fundi: Story of Ella Baker*. New York: Icarus Films, 1981.

Ransby, Barbara. *Ella Baker and the Black Freedom Movement: A Radical Democratic Vision*.
Chapel Hill, NC: University of North Carolina Press, 2003.

Scelfo, Julie. "On MLK Day, Honor the Mother of the Civil Rights Movement, Too." *TIME*.
January 16, 2017. time.com/4633460/mlk-day-ella-baker.

RUBY BRIDGES

Atkins, Stan. "Scene Outside Integrated Orleans School Described." *Lake Charles American
Press*. December 4, 1960. newspapers.com/clip/307588/ruby-bridges-william-frantz
-elementary.

Bridges, Ruby. *Ruby Bridges Goes to School: My True Story*. New York: Scholastic, 2003.

Bridges, Ruby. *This Is Your Time*. New York: Delacorte Press, 2020.

CLAUDETTE COLVIN

Hoose, Philip. *Claudette Colvin: Twice Toward Justice*. New York: Macmillan, 2009.

Mechanic, Michael. "Rosa Parks Didn't Act Alone: Meet Claudette Colvin." *Mother Jones*.
January 20, 2009. motherjones.com/politics/2009/01/rosa-parks-didnt-act-alone-meet
-claudette-colvin.

Waxman, Olivia B. "'I Was Not Going to Stand.' Rosa Parks Predecessors Recall Their History
-Making Acts of Resistance." *TIME*. March 2, 2020. time.com/5786220/claudette-colvin
-mary-louise-smith.

DOROTHY COTTON

Cotton, Dorothy. *If Your Back's Not Bent: The Role of the Citizenship Education Program in the Civil Rights Movement*. New York: Atria, 2012.

"Dorothy Cotton Oral History Interview." C-SPAN, July 25, 2011. Video, 1:48:54. c-span.org/video/?314517-1/dorothy-cotton-oral-history-interview.

"Dorothy Cotton—Short Biography." The Dorothy Cotton Institute. dorothycottoninstitute.org/about-dorothy-cotton/about-dorothy-cotton-biography.

Gillespie, Deanna M. "'First-Class' Citizenship Education in the Mississippi Delta, 1961–1965." *Journal of Southern History* 80, no. 1 (February 2014): 109–142. jstor.org/stable/23796845.

Sandomir, Richard. "Dorothy Cotton, Rights Champion and Close Aide to King, Dies at 88." *New York Times*. June 14, 2018. nytimes.com/2018/06/14/obituaries/dorothy-cotton-rights-champion-and-close-aide-to-king-dies-at-88.html.

Smith, Harrison. "Dorothy Cotton: Civil Rights Leader and Confidante to Martin Luther King." *Independent*. June 25, 2018. independent.co.uk/news/obituaries/dorothy-cotton-dead-civil-rights-movement-leader-martin-luther-king-a8399991.html.

FANNIE LOU HAMER

Blain, Keisha N. "Fannie Lou Hamer's Dauntless Fight for Black Americans' Right to Vote." *Smithsonian Magazine*. August 20, 2020. smithsonianmag.com/history/fannie-lou-hamers-dauntless-fight-for-black-americans-right-vote-180975610.

"Fannie Lou Hamer." *American Experience.* PBS. pbs.org/wgbh/americanexperience/features/freedomsummer-hamer.

Gilmore, Nicholas. "Fannie Lou Hamer's War on Voter Suppression." *Saturday Evening Post.* October 6, 2020. saturdayeveningpost.com/2020/10/fannie-lou-hamers-war-on-voter-suppression.

Michals, Debra, ed. "Fannie Lou Hamer." National Women's History Museum. womenshistory.org/education-resources/biographies/fannie-lou-hamer.

CORETTA SCOTT KING

King, Coretta Scott, and Barbara Reynolds. *My Life, My Love, My Legacy*. New York: Henry Holt, 2017.

Leifermann, Henry P. "Profession: Concert Singer, Freedom Movement Lecturer." *New York Times*. November 26, 1972. nytimes.com/1972/11/26/archives/-profession-concert-singer-freedom-movement-lecturer-ambiguous.html.

Theoharis, Jeanne. "Coretta Scott King and the Civil-Rights Movement's Hidden Women." *The Atlantic*. March 26, 2018. theatlantic.com/magazine/archive/2018/02/coretta-scott-king/552557.

DIANE NASH

Nash, Diane. "They Are the Ones Who Got Scared." In *Hands on the Freedom Plow: Personal Accounts by Women in SNCC*, edited by Faith S. Holsaert, Martha Prescod, Norman Noonan, Judy Richardson, Betty Garman Robinson, Jean Smith Young, and Dorothy M. Zellner. Urbana, IL: University of Illinois Press, 2010.

Nelson, Stanley, dir. *Freedom Riders*. New York: Firelight Media, 2010.

"Non-Violence and the Quest for Civil Rights." Transcript of keynote address by Diane Nash. John F. Kennedy Presidential Library and Museum. March 29, 2003. jfklibrary.org/events-and-awards/forums/past-forums/transcripts/non-violence-and-the-quest-for-civil-rights.

Waxman, Olivia. "Her Fight for Civil Rights Was Recognized During the March on Washington's Tribute to Women—But She Wasn't Actually There." *TIME*. September 17, 2019. time.com/5658736/march-on-washington-women-history.

ROSA PARKS

Parks, Rosa, and Jim Haskins. *Rosa Parks: My Story*. New York: Puffin Books, 1999.

Theoharis, Jeanne. *The Rebellious Life of Mrs. Rosa Parks*. Boston: Beacon Press, 2021.

BERNICE JOHNSON REAGON

Davis, Elizabeth Cooper. "Making Movement Sounds: The Cultural Organizing Behind the Freedom Songs of the Civil Rights Movement." PhD diss., Harvard University, 2017. nrs.harvard.edu/urn-3:HUL.InstRepos:39987965.

Hyder, Thomas. "The Legacy of Civil Rights Protest Music: Sweet Honey In The Rock's 'The Ballad Of Harry T. Moore.'" PhD diss., University of Central Florida, 2012. stars.library.ucf.edu/etd/2331.

Reagon, Bernice Johnson. "Music in the Civil Rights Movement." *American Experience*. PBS. 2006. pbs.org/wgbh/americanexperience/features/eyesontheprize-music-civil-rights-movement.

Reagon, Bernice Johnson. "Since I Laid My Burden Down." In *Hands on the Freedom Plow: Personal Accounts by Women in SNCC*, edited by Faith S. Holsaert, Martha Prescod, Norman Noonan, Judy Richardson, Betty Garman Robinson, Jean Smith Young, and Dorothy M. Zellner, 146. Urbana, IL: University of Illinois Press, 2010.

Reagon, Bernice Johnson "Songs of the Civil Rights Movement 1955–1965: A Study in Cultural History." PhD dissertation, Howard University, 1975: 6.

Reagon, Bernice Johnson. "Uncovered and Without Shelter, I Joined this Movement for Freedom." In *Hands on the Freedom Plow: Personal Accounts by Women in SNCC*, edited by Faith Holsaert, Martha Prescod, Norman Noonan, Judy Richardson, Betty Garman Robinson, Jean Smith Young, and Dorothy M. Zellner, 119. Urbana, IL: University of Illinois Press, 2010.

"Voices of the Civil Rights Movement: Black American Freedom Songs 1960-1966." Smithsonian Folkways Recordings. folkways.si.edu/voices-of-the-civil-rights-movement-black-american-freedom-songs-1960-1966/african-american-music-documentary-struggle-protest/album/smithsonian.

GLORIA RICHARDSON

Alexander, Keith L. "Gloria Richardson Pushed Aside a Bayonet as a '60s Civil Rights Activist. Now 98, She Wants the New Generation to Fight On." *Washington Post*. December 11, 2020. washingtonpost.com/local/gloria-richardson-civil-rights -blm/2020/12/10/b9cacdbe-29dd-11eb-8fa2-06e7cbb145c0_story.html.

Fitzgerald, Joseph R. *The Struggle Is Eternal: Gloria Richardson and Black Liberation*. Lexington, KY: University Press of Kentucky, 2018.

Rasmussen, Fred. "Gloria Richardson Dandridge: Led the Effort to Bring Civil Rights to Blacks in the 1960s." February 23, 1997. https://originalpeople.org/gloria-richardson -dandridge-led-effort-bring-civil-rights-blacks-60s/.

Richardson, Gloria. "Civil Rights Pioneer Gloria Richardson, 91, on How Women Were Silenced at 1963 March on Washington." Interview by Amy Goodman. *Democracy Now!* August 27, 2013. democracynow.org/2013/8/27/civil_rights_pioneer_gloria _richardson_91.

JO ANN ROBINSON

Robinson, Jo Ann. "Interview with Jo Ann Robinson." Washington University in St. Louis. August 27, 1979. repository.wustl.edu/concern/videos/37720f54k.

"Robinson, Jo Ann Gibson." Martin Luther King, Jr. Research and Education Institute. Stanford University. kinginstitute.stanford.edu/encyclopedia/robinson-jo-ann-gibson.

Robinson, Jo Ann. *The Montgomery Bus Boycott and the Woman Who Started It*. Knoxville: University of Tennessee Press, 1987.

SHEYANN WEBB

"Meet the Hero: Sheyann Webb." Lowell Milken Center for Unsung Heroes. lowellmilkencenter.org/programs/projects/view/pigtails-and-protests/hero.

"Selma 50th Anniversary: Youngest Marcher on Edmund Pettus Bridge Reflects." NBC News. March 6, 2015. nbcnews.com/storyline/selma-50th-anniversary/selma-anniversary-youngest-marcher-edmund-pettus-bridge-reflects-n318831.

Treadwell, David. "Debts to Dr. King: One Man So Touched Many Lives." *Los Angeles Times*. March 27, 1988. latimes.com/archives/la-xpm-1988-03-27-mn-403-story.html.

Webb, Sheyann. "Interview with Sheyann Webb." Washington University in St. Louis. December 6, 1985. repository.wustl.edu/concern/videos/v692t789g. (Transcription digital.wustl.edu/e/eop/eopweb/web0015.0942.109sheyannwebb.html.)

Webb, Sheyann, Rachel West Nelson, and Frank Sikora. *Selma, Lord, Selma: Girlhood Memories of the Civil-Rights Days*. Tuscaloosa, AL: University of Alabama Press, 1980.

FREEDOM MARCHERS

"Birmingham Campaign." Martin Luther King Jr. Research and Education Institute. Stanford University. kinginstitute.stanford.edu/encyclopedia/birmingham-campaign.

Clark, Alexis. "The Children's Crusade: When the Youth of Birmingham Marched for Justice." History.com. October 14, 2020. history.com/news/childrens-crusade-birmingham-civil-rights.

Hudson, Robert, and Robert Houston, dirs. *Mighty Times: The Children's March*. Montgomery, AL: Southern Poverty Law Center, 2004.

Hunter-Gault, Charlayne. "Fifty Years After the Birmingham Children's Crusade." *New Yorker*. May 2, 2013. newyorker.com/news/news-desk/fifty-years-after-the-birmingham-childrens-crusade.

EQUAL RIGHTS

W

FIGHT

DEM

FREEDOM NOW!!

JUS